To dear John,
Merry Christmas
2011
Lovingly,
Mary Ann

cottages

SWEETWATER
PRESS

Cottages
Copyright © 2008 by Cliff Road Books, Inc.
Produced by arrangement with Sweetwater Press

Pictures on pages 204-205 courtesy of Charleston, SC,
Convention and Visitors' Bureau

Cover photo: San Jose, California
© Douglas Keister

ISBN-13: 978-1-58173-731-8

Book and text by Patrick Covert
Printed in China

cottages

A cottage is more than a small house. It's a way of living large in a compact space. There is a strong element of home in every cottage. Because without exception, every cottage is a home: warm, inviting, full of personal style and architectural surprise. Even the definition of a cottage garden—a small garden full of a little bit of everything—makes the landscape of a cottage different from any other house.

Every country and culture brings its own special coloring to bear on its cottages. And yet whether located in the desert, the tropics, the mountains, or the plains, every cottage is connected by the common threads of efficiency, character, comfort, and charm. As you turn the pages of this book, travel through the world of cottages and absorb for yourself the details that make each of them, whether plain or fancy, a special tribute to a life full of loving thoughts, joyful times, and good living.

Belgium

San Diego, California

Prince Edward Island, Canada

Minnesota

Southern California

Nevada

Minnesota

Botswana

Chicago, Illinois

Montreal, Quebec

Michigan

Correze, France

Newport Beach, California

The Cotswolds, England

Brittany, France

Sweden

Virginia Dale, Colorado

Is there

anything

more

appealing

than a

cottage

tucked away

behind

a garden

gate...?

Gloucestershire, England

Australia

Long Island, New York

Spokane, Washington

Virginia

Montreal, Quebec

France

Halifax, Nova Scotia

Tilcara, Jujuy, Argentina

Norway

Finland

Algonquin Park, Ontario

Nevada

Scotland

Lofoten Islands, Norway

Berkmeer, Netherlands

Las Vegas, Nevada

Maine

Hegyszentmarton, Hungary

Evansville, Indiana

New Philadelphia, Ohio

California

Asheville, North Carolina

The cottage door
makes a statement
that simply says
"welcome."

Cornwall, England

Rimousski, Quebec

Opposite page - England

Whistler, British Columbia

Ireland

Cape Cod, Massachusetts

Lafayette, Indiana

Northumberland, England

Rustrel, Valcluse, France

To some
the cottage
is defined
not so
much as
what it is
but where
it is.

Macedonia

Saguenay, Quebec

England

The Cotswolds, England

Mozambique

Ireland

Ogden, Utah

Arizona

Lake Tahoe

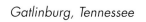

Gatlinburg, Tennessee

British Columbia

Opposite page - Goethe house, Weimar, Thuringia, Germany

Chicago, Illinois

The Netherlands

Virginia

Opposite page - New Jersey

Wales

Opposite page - Iowa

near Toronto, Canada

Australia

Opposite page - Birmingham, Alabama

Nebraska

Canada

Pays de la Loire, France

Villaluenga del Rosario, Cadiz, Spain

Avebury, England

Opposite page - Germany

Greece

Hungary

Germany

Italy

The Swiss Alps

British Columbia

Opposite page - Northern California

French Quarter, New Orleans

Opposite page - Istanbul, Turkey

Cayman Islands

Opposite page - Pensacola, Florida

Eagle County, Colorado

Opposite page - Key West, Florida

The Grand Bahamas

Cheshire, England

Quebec City, Quebec

The Grand Bahamas

Some would argue
there is no substitute
for the fresh air
of the sea,
and their cottage
simply wouldn't
breathe without it.

Island of Minorca

Koh Chang, Thailand

Palos Verdes, California

Previous page - Playa Hermosa, Costa Rica

Shenzen, China

Ontario

Most

cottages

have a

place of

magic

out back

or to

the side;

a spot

to relax

and

enjoy

one's

labors.

Opposite page - Queenslader, Australia

Russia

Lecce, Italy

Fairmont Hot Springs, British Columbia

Puna Cuna, Dominican Republic

Opposite page - Dominican Republic

Bristol, England

Turkey

Opposite page - Mexico

California

Venice Beach, California

Ebington, England

Puna Cuna, Dominican Republic

Opposite page - Dominican Republic

Bristol, England

Bonita Beach, Florida

Dovadola, Italy

Winston County, Alabama

Florida

Ontario

Quebec

Hamilton, New Jersey

Mihaesti, Romania

Birmingham, Alabama

Pasadena, California

Rockland, Maine

Rockford, Illinois

British Columbia

Opposite page - Lake Forest, Illinois

Louisiana

Seattle

California

Portugal

Opposite page - Pennsylvania

Santa Fe, New Mexico

Southern Germany

Toronto, Canada

Switzerland

Nevada

Florida

San Diego County, California

Mercer County, New Jersey

Russia

Monmouthshire, Wales

Hingham, Massachusetts

Charleston, South Carolina

British Columbia

Outer Banks, North Carolina